Healthy Life Rules:

The Ultimate Guide to Living a Healthy Life

Table of Contents

Introduction

As the sun sets over the horizon, a sense of unease settles in the air. The world is changing rapidly, and we're all struggling to keep up. Our lives have become increasingly busy and chaotic, leaving little room for self-care and personal growth. But what if I told you there was a way to take control of your life and find happiness amidst the chaos? What if I told you that the secrets to living a fulfilled and joyful life lie within these pages? Welcome to a journey of self-discovery and personal growth, where you'll uncover the tools to create a life that is filled with purpose, meaning, and happiness. But be warned - this journey isn't for the faint-hearted. It will challenge you, push you out of your comfort zone, and require you to confront the parts of yourself that you may have been avoiding. But if you're willing to take that first step, to be vulnerable, and to embrace the unknown, then I promise that the reward will be worth it. So, are you ready to embark on a journey of a lifetime? Let's begin.

Chapter 1: Make Healthy Eating a Habit

In this chapter, we'll explore the importance of healthy eating and how to make it a habit. We'll discuss the benefits of a balanced diet and provide practical tips on how to incorporate healthy foods into your daily routine. We'll also bust common myths around healthy eating and provide guidance on how to create a sustainable and enjoyable diet.

Healthy eating is a vital component of a healthy lifestyle. It provides the necessary nutrients, vitamins, and minerals that our bodies need to function optimally. A balanced diet can help prevent chronic diseases such as heart disease, diabetes, and obesity, and promote longevity and overall well-being.

In this chapter, we'll delve into the importance of healthy eating and provide practical tips on how to make it a habit. We'll start by exploring the components of a balanced diet, including macronutrients, such as carbohydrates, proteins, and fats, and micronutrients, such as vitamins and minerals. We'll also discuss the importance of hydration and the role of fiber in maintaining a healthy digestive system.

We'll then move on to practical tips on how to incorporate healthy foods into your daily routine. We'll explore the benefits of meal planning, mindful eating, and healthy snacking. We'll also provide guidance on how to read food labels, choose healthier options when eating out, and how to cook healthy meals at home.

We'll also address common myths around healthy eating, such as the belief that healthy foods are tasteless or expensive. We'll discuss how to create a sustainable and enjoyable diet that includes a variety of foods that you enjoy. We'll explore the concept of "crowding out" unhealthy foods with healthier options and the benefits of mindful indulgence.

Finally, we'll provide tips on how to overcome common barriers to healthy eating, such as lack of time, motivation, or knowledge. We'll discuss the benefits of seeking support from family, friends, or a registered dietitian, and how to set realistic goals and track your progress.

To further elaborate on the importance of healthy eating, it's essential to understand that what we eat not only affects our physical health but also our mental health. Research has shown that a diet high in processed foods and sugar can lead to inflammation in the body, which is linked to the development of mental health disorders such as depression and anxiety.

On the other hand, a diet rich in fruits, vegetables, whole grains, and healthy fats such as omega-3 fatty acids can have a protective effect on mental health. These foods contain nutrients that help support brain function, improve mood, and reduce inflammation.

Incorporating healthy foods into your diet doesn't have to be complicated or restrictive. It's about finding a balance that works for you and making small changes over time. For example, start by adding more fruits and vegetables to your meals or swapping out processed snacks for whole food options.

It's also important to note that healthy eating doesn't have to be expensive. Eating seasonally and locally can help reduce costs, and buying in bulk and planning meals ahead of time can also help save money. Additionally, cooking at home instead of eating out can not only be more cost-effective but also allow for more control over the ingredients used in your meals.

In conclusion,, making healthy eating a habit is a crucial step towards living a healthy life. By following the tips and guidelines outlined in this chapter, you can adopt a balanced and sustainable diet that nourishes your body and promotes overall well-being. So, start today and make healthy eating a lifelong habit.

Making healthy eating a habit is a vital component of a healthy lifestyle. By incorporating more whole, nutrient-dense foods into your diet and making small, sustainable changes over time, you can support both your physical and mental well-being. Remember, healthy eating is not about perfection but progress, so start small and keep making progress towards a healthier you

Chapter 2: Exercise for a Strong Body and Mind

Exercise is crucial for maintaining a healthy body and mind. In this chapter, we'll explore the benefits of regular exercise and provide practical tips on how to get started. We'll discuss different types of exercise, including strength training, cardio, and yoga, and provide guidance on how to create a workout plan that works for you.

Regular exercise is an essential aspect of a healthy lifestyle. It can help prevent chronic diseases such as heart disease, diabetes, and obesity, and promote overall physical and mental well-being. In this chapter, we'll delve into the benefits of regular exercise and provide practical tips on how to get started.

First and foremost, we'll explore the various benefits of exercise, which include maintaining a healthy weight, improving cardiovascular health, strengthening bones and muscles, and reducing the risk of chronic diseases. Additionally, regular exercise has been shown to have a positive effect on mental health, reducing symptoms of anxiety and depression, and improving cognitive function.

Next, we'll discuss different types of exercise, including strength training, cardio, and yoga. Strength training helps build muscle mass and increase metabolism, while cardio exercises such as running, cycling, or swimming improve cardiovascular health and endurance. Yoga is an excellent form of exercise that promotes flexibility, balance, and mindfulness.

We'll provide guidance on how to create a workout plan that works for you, including setting realistic goals and finding exercises that you enjoy. It's essential to find a balance between challenging yourself and not pushing too hard, as overexertion can lead to injury or burnout. We'll also discuss the importance of warm-ups and cool-downs, as well as how to properly use equipment and weights.

Additionally, we'll explore ways to stay motivated and consistent with your exercise routine. Setting specific and achievable goals, finding an accountability partner, and incorporating variety into your workouts can help keep you on track. We'll also address common barriers to exercise, such as lack of time, energy, or access to equipment or facilities, and provide alternative solutions.

Finally, we'll discuss the importance of rest and recovery in your exercise routine. Rest days are essential for allowing your body to recover and reduce the risk of injury. Stretching and foam rolling can also help prevent muscle soreness and tightness.

It's also important to note that exercise doesn't have to be complicated or time-consuming. Even small amounts of physical activity, such as taking a walk or doing a few minutes of stretching, can have significant health benefits. Finding ways to incorporate movement into your daily routine, such as taking the stairs instead of the elevator or doing a quick workout during your lunch break, can also help increase your overall activity level.

Another key factor in sticking to an exercise routine is finding activities that you enjoy. Whether it's running, dancing, swimming, or hiking, there are many different ways to get your heart rate up and challenge your body. Experimenting with different types of exercise and finding a community of like-minded individuals can also help make exercise more enjoyable and sustainable.

It's also important to remember that everyone's body is different, and what works for one person may not work for another. It's essential to listen to your body and adjust your exercise routine accordingly. If you're experiencing pain or discomfort during exercise, it's important to consult with a healthcare professional to ensure that you're not causing harm.

It's worth noting that consistency is key when it comes to exercise. While it's great to get a workout in every once in a while, it's the regular, consistent exercise that truly leads to improved health and fitness. It's recommended that adults get at least 150 minutes of moderate-intensity aerobic exercise or 75 minutes of vigorous-intensity aerobic exercise per week, spread out over at least three days. Strength training should also be included in your exercise routine at least twice a week.

To help ensure that you're meeting these guidelines, it can be helpful to track your workouts and progress. Whether you use a fitness app, a workout journal, or simply mark your workouts on a calendar, tracking your exercise can help keep you motivated and accountable.

Another important aspect of exercise is fueling your body with proper nutrition. Eating a balanced diet that includes plenty of protein, healthy fats, and complex carbohydrates can help support your exercise routine and improve your overall health. It's also important to stay hydrated by drinking plenty of water before, during, and after exercise.

Lastly, it's important to remember that exercise is not a one-size-fits-all solution. What works for one person may not work for another, and it's important to find an exercise routine that fits your individual needs, preferences, and lifestyle. Whether you prefer to work out alone or with a group, in a gym or in the great outdoors, there are many different ways to get active and stay healthy.

In conclusion, exercise is a crucial component of a healthy lifestyle. By finding activities that you enjoy and creating a workout plan that works for you, you can reap the many physical and mental benefits of regular exercise. Remember, exercise doesn't have to be complicated or time-consuming, and even small amounts of physical activity can make a significant difference in your overall health and well-being.

Exercise is a crucial component of a healthy lifestyle, and finding a workout routine that works for you can lead to improved physical and mental health. By staying consistent, tracking your progress, fueling your body with proper nutrition, and finding an exercise routine that fits your individual needs, you can achieve your fitness goals and improve your overall well-being.

Regular exercise is a crucial aspect of a healthy lifestyle. By finding exercises that you enjoy and creating a workout plan that works for you, you can reap the many physical and mental benefits of regular exercise. So, start today and make exercise a part of your daily routine for a strong body and mind.

Chapter 3: Prioritize Sleep for Optimal Health

Sleep is often overlooked but is essential for overall health and well-being. In this chapter, we'll explore the benefits of good sleep and provide practical tips on how to improve your sleep quality. We'll discuss the importance of a consistent sleep schedule, creating a sleep-friendly environment, and addressing common sleep disorders.

Getting a good night's sleep is essential for maintaining optimal health and well-being. It's during sleep that our bodies repair and regenerate, and lack of sleep can have a significant impact on our physical and mental health.

One of the most important factors in getting quality sleep is maintaining a consistent sleep schedule. This means going to bed and waking up at the same time every day, even on weekends. Our bodies thrive on routine, and a consistent sleep schedule can help regulate our body's internal clock, making it easier to fall asleep and wake up feeling refreshed.

Creating a sleep-friendly environment is also crucial for getting quality sleep. This means keeping your bedroom cool, quiet, and dark, and minimizing distractions like electronics and clutter. Investing in a comfortable mattress and pillows can also help ensure a comfortable and restful sleep.

Another important aspect of good sleep is addressing common sleep disorders, such as sleep apnea and insomnia. These conditions can significantly impact sleep quality and overall health, and it's important to consult with a healthcare professional if you suspect you may be suffering from a sleep disorder.

In addition to these practical tips, there are also lifestyle changes you can make to improve your sleep quality. For example, avoiding caffeine and alcohol before bed, getting regular exercise, and practicing relaxation techniques like meditation and deep breathing can all help promote restful sleep.

Prioritizing sleep is essential for maintaining optimal health and well-being. By maintaining a consistent sleep schedule, creating a sleep-friendly environment, addressing common sleep disorders, and making lifestyle changes to promote restful sleep, you can improve your sleep quality and reap the many physical and mental benefits of good sleep.

It's important to note that the amount of sleep required can vary from person to person, but most adults require between 7-9 hours of sleep per night. Consistently getting less than this amount of sleep can have negative impacts on our health, including increased risk of obesity, diabetes, cardiovascular disease, and mental health disorders.

One common myth around sleep is that we can "catch up" on missed sleep on the weekends. However, studies have shown that irregular sleep patterns, such as sleeping in on the weekends, can disrupt our body's internal clock and actually make it more difficult to fall asleep and wake up during the week. Maintaining a consistent sleep schedule throughout the week is the best way to ensure good sleep quality and overall health.

If you struggle with getting quality sleep, there are many resources available to help. Your healthcare provider can offer guidance and treatment options for sleep disorders, and there are many apps and tools available to track and improve your sleep quality.

Prioritizing sleep is an essential component of a healthy lifestyle. By maintaining a consistent sleep schedule, creating a sleep-friendly environment, addressing sleep disorders, and making lifestyle changes to promote restful sleep, you can improve your sleep quality and overall health and well-being.

It's important to note that the benefits of good sleep extend beyond physical health. Sleep also plays a crucial role in mental health, with lack of sleep contributing to increased risk of depression, anxiety, and other mental health disorders. Additionally, good sleep has been linked to improved cognitive function, including better memory and concentration.

In contrast, chronic sleep deprivation can lead to impaired cognitive function, including decreased attention and problem-solving abilities. This can impact performance at work or school and overall quality of life.

It's also worth noting that sleep quality can be impacted by external factors, such as stress and anxiety. In these cases, it may be helpful to incorporate stress-reducing practices into your daily routine, such as mindfulness meditation or yoga, to promote better sleep.

In conclusion, prioritizing sleep is crucial for maintaining optimal health and well-being, both physically and mentally. By incorporating the practical tips and lifestyle changes outlined in this chapter, you can improve your sleep quality and reap the many benefits of good sleep.

Chapter 4: Manage Stress for Mental Health

Stress is a common factor in modern life and can have negative impacts on mental health. In this chapter, we'll explore the effects of stress on the body and mind and provide practical tips on how to manage stress effectively. We'll discuss different stress management techniques, such as meditation, deep breathing, and exercise, and provide guidance on how to create a stress-management plan that works for you.

Stress is a natural response to challenging or overwhelming situations, but chronic stress can have negative impacts on both our physical and mental health. Long-term stress can contribute to a range of health issues, including high blood pressure, cardiovascular disease, and mental health disorders such as anxiety and depression.

Fortunately, there are many effective strategies for managing stress. One approach is to identify and address the sources of stress in your life. This may involve setting boundaries with work or personal commitments, seeking support from loved ones, or making lifestyle changes to promote relaxation and self-care.

In addition to addressing the root causes of stress, there are many techniques for managing stress in the moment. Mindfulness meditation and deep breathing exercises are effective tools for reducing stress and promoting relaxation. Exercise, particularly activities like yoga or tai chi, can also be effective for reducing stress and promoting a sense of calm.

It's worth noting that not all stress is bad. In fact, a moderate amount of stress can be motivating and energizing. However, it's important to find a balance between healthy stress and chronic stress, and to develop effective strategies for managing stress when it becomes overwhelming.

Managing stress is an essential component of a healthy lifestyle. By identifying and addressing the sources of stress in your life, incorporating stress-reducing practices into your daily routine, and finding a healthy balance between healthy stress and chronic stress, you can promote optimal mental health and well-being.

It's important to note that stress management techniques are not one-size-fits-all. What works for one person may not be effective for another, so it's important to experiment with different techniques to find what works best for you.

In addition, it's important to develop a proactive approach to stress management. Rather than waiting until stress becomes overwhelming, make stress management a regular part of your self-care routine. This may involve scheduling regular breaks throughout the day, practicing mindfulness or deep breathing exercises at set times, or engaging in regular physical activity to promote relaxation and stress reduction.

Finally, it's worth noting that while stress management can be effective in reducing the negative impacts of stress, it's not always possible to eliminate stress altogether. In these cases, it's important to develop resilience and coping skills to help manage stress when it arises. This may involve seeking support from loved ones, engaging in hobbies or activities that promote relaxation and joy, or seeking professional support from a mental health provider.

Managing stress is essential for promoting optimal mental health and well-being. By identifying and addressing sources of stress, developing effective stress management strategies, and building resilience and coping skills, you can improve your ability to manage stress and lead a happier, healthier life.

It's important to remember that stress is a natural part of life, and that some stress can be healthy and motivating. However, when stress becomes chronic or overwhelming, it can have negative impacts on both our physical and mental health. That's why it's important to take proactive steps to manage stress and promote well-being.

There are many different stress management techniques to choose from, so it's important to find what works best for you. Some people find that physical activity, such as going for a run or practicing yoga, is an effective way to manage stress. Others may prefer mindfulness practices, such as meditation or deep breathing exercises. Still others may find that engaging in creative activities, such as painting or writing, is a helpful way to manage stress and promote relaxation.

In addition to these individual strategies, it's also important to address sources of stress in your life. This may involve setting boundaries with work or personal commitments, seeking support from loved ones, or making lifestyle changes to promote relaxation and self-care.

Finally, if you find that stress is significantly impacting your daily life or ability to function, it may be worth seeking professional support from a mental health provider. They can help you develop personalized strategies for managing stress and promote overall mental health and well-being.

In conclusion, managing stress is an essential part of living a healthy life. By identifying effective stress management strategies, addressing sources of stress, and seeking professional support when needed, you can promote optimal mental health and well-being and lead a happier, healthier life.

Chapter 5: Build Strong Relationships for a Healthy Life

Healthy relationships are essential for a fulfilling life. In this chapter, we'll explore the importance of social connections and provide practical tips on how to build and maintain strong relationships. We'll discuss the benefits of positive relationships on mental and physical health and provide guidance on how to improve communication skills and establish healthy boundaries.

Human beings are social creatures, and maintaining positive relationships with others is an important aspect of overall health and well-being. In fact, studies have shown that people who have strong social connections tend to live longer, have better physical and mental health, and experience greater levels of happiness and life satisfaction.

Building and maintaining strong relationships can take effort, but the benefits are well worth it. One important aspect of healthy relationships is effective communication. This means being able to express your thoughts and feelings clearly and honestly, while also being a good listener and showing empathy for others.

Establishing healthy boundaries is another important aspect of building strong relationships. This means being able to set limits on what you are comfortable with and respecting the boundaries of others. By setting and respecting boundaries, you can create a sense of safety and respect within your relationships, which can promote greater trust and intimacy.

It's also important to recognize that relationships can be complex and may require different approaches depending on the individual and the situation. For example, building a romantic relationship may involve different strategies than building a friendship or a professional relationship.

Ultimately, building strong relationships requires a willingness to be open, honest, and vulnerable with others, while also showing respect, empathy, and compassion. By prioritizing social connections and working to build and maintain positive relationships, you can promote optimal mental and physical health and lead a fulfilling and happy life.

In addition to effective communication and establishing healthy boundaries, there are other important strategies for building strong relationships. One key strategy is to prioritize quality time with loved ones. This means carving out dedicated time to spend with the people who are important to you, whether it's through shared hobbies, activities, or simply spending time together.

Another important strategy is to practice forgiveness and understanding. No relationship is perfect, and conflicts and misunderstandings can arise. However, by practicing forgiveness and striving to understand the other person's perspective, you can create a sense of empathy and compassion that can strengthen your bond and lead to greater intimacy.

It's also important to be a good listener and to show interest in the lives of those around you. This means actively listening to what others have to say, asking questions, and showing genuine interest in their thoughts and feelings. By doing so, you can create a sense of connection and belonging that can be a powerful source of support and comfort.

Finally, it's important to recognize the importance of self-care in building strong relationships. This means taking care of your own physical and mental health needs, such as getting enough sleep, exercising regularly, and managing stress effectively. By taking care of yourself, you can show up as a better partner, friend, or family member and build stronger, more fulfilling relationships.

Overall, building strong relationships is a key aspect of living a healthy life. By prioritizing communication, healthy boundaries, quality time, forgiveness and understanding, active listening, and self-care, you can build strong and fulfilling relationships that promote optimal physical and mental health.

Chapter 6: Create a Healthy Environment

The environment we live in has a significant impact on our health and well-being. In this chapter, we'll explore the importance of a healthy environment and provide practical tips on how to create one. We'll discuss the impact of air quality, lighting, and noise on health and provide guidance on how to create a healthy living space.

Creating a healthy environment is essential for optimal health and well-being. There are many factors that contribute to a healthy environment, including air quality, lighting, and noise levels. By optimizing these factors, you can create a living space that supports your physical and mental health.

One important aspect of a healthy environment is air quality. Poor air quality can have negative impacts on respiratory health and can exacerbate allergies and asthma. To improve air quality, consider using an air purifier or opening windows to improve ventilation. You can also incorporate plants into your living space, as they can help filter pollutants from the air.

Another important aspect of a healthy environment is lighting. Exposure to natural light can improve mood and productivity, while excessive exposure to artificial light can disrupt circadian rhythms and affect sleep quality. To optimize lighting, try to maximize natural light in your living space and avoid excessive exposure to screens and artificial light sources in the evening.

Noise levels can also have a significant impact on health and well-being. Excessive noise can lead to stress, anxiety, and sleep disturbances. To reduce noise levels in your living space, consider using noise-cancelling headphones, soundproofing walls or windows, or creating a designated quiet space in your home.

In addition to optimizing air quality, lighting, and noise levels, there are other strategies for creating a healthy living space. These include incorporating natural elements, such as plants and natural materials, into your living space, minimizing clutter and promoting organization, and creating a space that supports relaxation and stress reduction.

Creating a healthy environment is an important aspect of living a healthy life. By optimizing air quality, lighting, and noise levels, incorporating natural elements, and promoting relaxation and stress reduction, you can create a living space that supports your physical and mental health and promotes optimal well-being.

In addition to the physical aspects of creating a healthy environment, it is also important to consider the social and cultural environment. Surrounding yourself with positive and supportive people can have a significant impact on mental health and well-being. It's important to create a social network of people who uplift and support you and to avoid toxic relationships that drain your energy and contribute to stress and negative emotions.

Cultural environment can also play a role in overall health and well-being. Being part of a culture that values health and wellness can be motivating and can provide a supportive environment for making healthy choices. Conversely, being part of a culture that promotes unhealthy habits can be a barrier to living a healthy life. It's important to be aware of the cultural factors that influence your lifestyle choices and to seek out cultural environments that support your health and well-being.

Finally, creating a healthy environment also involves being mindful of the impact of our actions on the environment around us. Taking steps to reduce our carbon footprint, such as using public transportation, reducing waste, and conserving energy, can have a positive impact on both the environment and our own well-being.

Creating a healthy environment involves optimizing physical factors such as air quality, lighting, and noise levels, as well as surrounding ourselves with positive and supportive social networks, being mindful of cultural factors, and taking action to protect the environment. By creating a healthy living space and promoting a healthy cultural and social environment, we can support our physical, mental, and emotional well-being and live a fulfilling and healthy life.

It's important to note that creating a healthy environment is not a one-time task, but an ongoing process. It requires continuous effort and attention to maintain a healthy living space and lifestyle. Regular maintenance of your home environment, such as cleaning and organizing, can have a positive impact on mental well-being and reduce stress.

In addition to maintaining a healthy environment, it's important to take proactive steps to prevent health problems. This can include things like regularly scheduled doctor visits, immunizations, and health screenings. It's also important to be aware of potential health hazards in the environment, such as air pollution, toxins, and hazardous chemicals, and take steps to minimize exposure.

In conclusion,, creating a healthy environment involves taking a holistic approach to health and well-being. By paying attention to all aspects of our environment, including physical, social, cultural, and environmental factors, we can create a supportive and healthy living space that promotes overall wellness.

Mindfulness is a technique that can help you focus on the present moment and improve mental clarity. In this chapter, we'll explore the benefits of mindfulness for mental health and provide practical tips on how to practice mindfulness. We'll discuss different mindfulness techniques, such as meditation, deep breathing, and body scans, and provide guidance on how to incorporate mindfulness into your daily routine.

Mindfulness is a practice that can be easily integrated into daily life and can have numerous benefits for mental health. Studies have shown that mindfulness can reduce symptoms of depression, anxiety, and stress, and improve overall well-being. It involves focusing attention on the present moment and becoming aware of one's thoughts, feelings, and physical sensations without judgment.

One of the most common mindfulness practices is meditation, which involves sitting quietly and focusing on your breath or a specific object. Meditation can help reduce stress and anxiety, improve concentration, and promote a sense of calm and relaxation. Other mindfulness techniques include deep breathing exercises, body scans, and mindful movement practices such as yoga or tai chi.

In this chapter, we'll explore the benefits of mindfulness for mental clarity and provide practical tips on how to incorporate mindfulness into your daily routine. We'll also discuss the common challenges people face when starting a mindfulness practice, such as difficulty focusing or feeling restless, and provide guidance on how to overcome them.

In addition to formal mindfulness practices, it's important to cultivate mindfulness in daily activities such as eating, walking, and communicating with others. This can involve paying attention to sensations, thoughts, and emotions as they arise and developing a non-judgmental awareness of them.

Practicing mindfulness can have a positive impact on mental health and well-being. By incorporating mindfulness practices into daily life and cultivating present-moment awareness, we can improve mental clarity, reduce stress, and enhance overall well-being.

In addition to reducing stress and anxiety, practicing mindfulness has also been linked to improvements in cognitive function and overall mental clarity. By focusing on the present moment and being fully present in the task at hand, mindfulness can help to improve concentration, memory, and decision-making skills.

There are various mindfulness techniques that you can practice to help improve your mental clarity. One technique is to practice mindful breathing, where you focus on your breath and bring your attention back to your breath whenever your mind wanders. Another technique is body scanning, where you focus on each part of your body in turn and pay attention to any sensations that you may be feeling.

Incorporating mindfulness into your daily routine can be as simple as taking a few minutes each day to practice deep breathing exercises or meditate. You can also practice mindfulness while engaging in other activities, such as going for a walk or doing household chores. By bringing your attention fully to the task at hand and focusing on the present moment, you can cultivate a greater sense of mental clarity and well-being.

Mindfulness is not just about being present in the moment, but also about accepting your thoughts and emotions without judgment. By practicing non-judgmental awareness, you can learn to observe your thoughts and feelings without getting caught up in them or becoming overwhelmed.

One technique for practicing non-judgmental awareness is to simply observe your thoughts and feelings without trying to change them. Instead of judging yourself or getting caught up in negative self-talk, try to observe your thoughts and emotions with curiosity and compassion. This can help you to develop a greater sense of self-awareness and understanding, and ultimately lead to improved mental health and well-being.

In addition to practicing mindfulness on your own, you can also participate in mindfulness-based programs such as mindfulness-based stress reduction (MBSR) or mindfulness-based cognitive therapy (MBCT). These programs typically involve a combination of mindfulness meditation, gentle yoga, and group discussions, and can help you to develop a more regular mindfulness practice and connect with others who share your goals.

By incorporating mindfulness into your daily routine, you can cultivate a greater sense of mental clarity, improve cognitive function, and develop a greater sense of self-awareness and compassion. With practice and patience, you can make mindfulness a habit and reap the many benefits that it has to offer.

Life Harmful habits such as smoking, excessive alcohol consumption, and drug abuse can have a significant impact on overall health and well-being. In this chapter, we'll explore the effects of harmful habits on the body and mind and provide practical tips on how to avoid them. We'll discuss the benefits of quitting smoking, reducing alcohol consumption, and seeking help for drug abuse.

Harmful habits can lead to serious health problems, both physical and mental. In this chapter, we'll explore the importance of avoiding harmful habits and provide practical tips on how to make positive changes.

Smoking is one of the most significant causes of preventable disease and death worldwide. It increases the risk of lung cancer, heart disease, and stroke, among other health problems. Quitting smoking can be challenging, but there are many resources available to help you quit, such as nicotine replacement therapy, counseling, and support groups. We'll discuss the benefits of quitting smoking and provide guidance on how to develop a quit plan that works for you.

Excessive alcohol consumption can lead to a range of health problems, such as liver disease, high blood pressure, and cancer. Drinking in moderation is generally safe for most people, but if you're struggling to control your alcohol intake, seeking help is essential. We'll discuss the benefits of reducing alcohol consumption and provide guidance on how to seek help if you need it.

Drug abuse can have devastating effects on physical and mental health, as well as relationships and work performance. Seeking help for drug abuse is crucial to prevent long-term damage to health and well-being. We'll discuss the importance of seeking professional help for drug abuse and provide guidance on how to find the right treatment program.

In this chapter, we'll emphasize the importance of avoiding harmful habits and making positive changes for a healthy life. We'll provide practical tips and resources to help you quit smoking, reduce alcohol consumption, and seek help for drug abuse. By making positive changes, you can improve your overall health and well-being and live a fulfilling life.

Harmful habits, such as smoking, excessive alcohol consumption, and drug abuse, can have a significant impact on overall health and well-being. In this chapter, we'll explore the effects of harmful habits on the body and mind and provide practical tips on how to avoid them.

Smoking

Smoking is one of the most harmful habits for overall health. It increases the risk of lung cancer, heart disease, stroke, and respiratory diseases. It can also damage your teeth and gums, cause bad breath, and lead to premature aging of the skin.

If you're a smoker, quitting can be challenging, but it's one of the best things you can do for your health. There are several ways to quit smoking, including cold turkey, nicotine replacement therapy, and medications. It's essential to find a method that works for you and seek support from family, friends, or a healthcare provider.

Excessive Alcohol Consumption

Drinking alcohol in moderation is not necessarily harmful, but excessive alcohol consumption can have negative effects on health. It increases the risk of liver disease, heart disease, and certain cancers. It can also lead to accidents, injuries, and addiction.

If you choose to drink alcohol, it's essential to do so in moderation. The recommended limits are one drink per day for women and two drinks per day for men. If you're struggling with alcohol addiction, seeking professional help is essential.

Drug Abuse

Drug abuse can have severe physical and mental health consequences. It can lead to addiction, overdose, and long-term damage to organs such as the liver and brain. It can also have negative effects on relationships, work, and finances.

If you're struggling with drug abuse, seeking help from a healthcare professional is essential. Treatment options include detoxification, behavioral therapy, and medication-assisted therapy.

In conclusion, harmful habits can have a significant impact on overall health and well-being. Quitting smoking, drinking alcohol in moderation, and avoiding drug abuse can lead to a healthier and happier life. Seeking professional help is essential if you're struggling with addiction or need support to quit harmful habits

Chapter 9: Find Joy in Life for Emotional

Health Finding joy in life is essential for emotional health and well-being. In this chapter, we'll explore the benefits of positive emotions and provide practical tips on how to find joy in life. We'll discuss the impact of gratitude, kindness, and humor on emotional health and provide guidance on how to incorporate these into daily life.

In addition to the physical and mental aspects of health, emotional health is also important for overall well-being. Finding joy in life can have a significant impact on emotional health and can help to reduce stress and improve mood.

In this chapter, we'll explore the benefits of positive emotions and provide practical tips on how to find joy in life. We'll begin by discussing the impact of gratitude on emotional health. Gratitude involves recognizing and appreciating the good things in life, both big and small. Practicing gratitude regularly has been linked to improved emotional health, increased happiness, and reduced stress. We'll provide guidance on how to incorporate gratitude into daily life, such as through journaling or expressing gratitude to others.

Kindness is another key aspect of finding joy in life. Acts of kindness towards others, even small ones, have been shown to boost happiness and improve emotional well-being. We'll provide practical tips on how to incorporate kindness into daily life, such as through volunteering or small acts of kindness towards family and friends.

Humor is also an important aspect of finding joy in life. Laughter has been shown to reduce stress, boost mood, and even improve the immune system. We'll provide guidance on how to incorporate humor into daily life, such as through watching comedy or spending time with friends who make you laugh.

Finally, we'll discuss the importance of finding activities that bring joy and fulfillment. Engaging in activities that bring a sense of purpose and satisfaction can help to improve emotional well-being. We'll provide practical tips on how to identify activities that bring joy and incorporate them into daily life.

Finding joy in life is an important aspect of emotional health and can have a significant impact on overall well-being. By incorporating gratitude, kindness, humor, and fulfilling activities into daily life, it is possible to find joy and improve emotional health.

Finding joy in life is not always easy, especially when we are faced with challenges and hardships. However, it is essential for our emotional health and well-being. When we experience positive emotions, such as joy, gratitude, and love, it not only feels good but also has numerous health benefits. Positive emotions can boost our immune system, lower stress levels, and improve our mental health.

One way to find joy in life is to practice gratitude. Gratitude involves recognizing and appreciating the good things in our lives, no matter how small they may be. This can be as simple as taking a few minutes each day to reflect on the things we are thankful for, such as our health, family, friends, or a beautiful sunset.

Another way to find joy in life is to practice kindness. Acts of kindness not only benefit others but also bring us joy and a sense of purpose. This can be as simple as holding the door open for someone, offering a compliment, or volunteering at a local charity.

Lastly, humor is an excellent way to find joy in life. Laughter has been shown to have numerous health benefits, such as reducing stress and improving our mood. Finding humor in everyday situations can help us to lighten up and find joy in life.

Incorporating these practices into our daily lives can help us to find joy and improve our emotional health. It's important to remember that finding joy is not always about big moments or achievements, but often about the small moments and simple pleasures that make life worth living.

Chapter 10: Continuously Learn for Personal Growth

Continuously learning is essential for personal growth and development. In this chapter, we'll explore the benefits of learning and provide practical tips on how to continuously learn. We'll discuss the impact of learning on mental health, career growth, and overall well-being and provide guidance on how to incorporate learning into daily life.

Continuous learning is a vital aspect of personal growth and development. In this chapter, we'll explore the benefits of learning and provide practical tips on how to continuously learn throughout life.

Learning is a lifelong process that can help improve mental health, career growth, and overall well-being. It allows individuals to gain new knowledge, develop new skills, and broaden their perspective. Continuous learning can help individuals adapt to changes in their personal and professional lives and remain competitive in the job market.

One of the most effective ways to continuously learn is to set learning goals. This involves identifying areas of interest and creating a plan to learn more about them. For example, if an individual wants to learn more about digital marketing, they can set a goal to read books on the topic, take online courses, and attend seminars or workshops.

Another way to continuously learn is to take advantage of online resources. The internet provides a wealth of information, including free online courses, podcasts, and blogs. These resources can help individuals learn new skills, gain knowledge on a wide range of topics, and stay up-to-date on current events.

Additionally, individuals can consider joining a community of learners. This can be in the form of a book club, study group, or online community. Joining a community of learners provides an opportunity to share ideas, ask questions, and learn from others.

Finally, it is important to cultivate a growth mindset. This involves embracing challenges, viewing failures as opportunities for growth, and continuously seeking new learning experiences. With a growth mindset, individuals can approach learning with enthusiasm and openness, making it an enjoyable and fulfilling experience.

Continuous learning is essential for personal growth and development. By setting learning goals, taking advantage of online resources, joining a community of learners, and cultivating a growth mindset, individuals can continuously learn and improve their knowledge, skills, and overall well-being.

practical tips on how to continuously learn

1. Choose topics that interest you: When deciding what to learn, focus on topics that interest you. It will make the learning process more enjoyable, and you'll be more likely to stick with it.

2. Use various sources: There are many ways to learn, including books, online courses, podcasts, and videos. Don't limit yourself to one source; try to incorporate various methods of learning to keep things interesting.

3. Set goals: Set specific learning goals for yourself, such as reading one book a month or completing a specific course. Having a goal to work towards can help you stay motivated and focused.

4. Embrace failure: Don't be afraid to fail when learning something new. Failure is a natural part of the learning process and can help you grow and improve.

5. Share what you've learned: Teaching others what you've learned is a great way to solidify your understanding of a topic and help others at the same

time. Look for opportunities to share your knowledge with others, whether it's through volunteering or teaching a class.

6. Stay curious: Cultivate a sense of curiosity about the world around you. Ask questions and seek out new experiences. Embracing a sense of curiosity can help you maintain a lifelong love of learning.

The impact of learning on mental health is significant. Learning new skills and knowledge can help boost self-esteem, confidence, and overall well-being. Additionally, continuous learning can help individuals stay engaged and stimulated, which can contribute to a sense of purpose and fulfillment.

In terms of career growth, continuous learning is crucial for remaining competitive in the job market and staying relevant in a rapidly evolving economy. It can help individuals develop new skills and expand their knowledge base, which can lead to career advancement opportunities and higher earning potential.

Overall, this chapter emphasizes the importance of making learning a lifelong habit and I encourages individuals to embrace new experiences and challenges as part of their personal growth and development journey

Chapter 11: Seek Professional Help When Needed

Sometimes, despite our best efforts, we may still face challenges that require professional help. In this chapter, we'll explore the benefits of seeking professional help and provide guidance on how to find the right professional. We'll discuss the impact of therapy, medication, and other forms of professional help on mental health and overall well-being.

Seeking professional help when needed is an important step towards improving mental and physical health. In this chapter, we'll delve into the reasons why seeking professional help is crucial and provide guidance on how to find the right professional.

There are many situations where seeking professional help is necessary. For example, if you're experiencing symptoms of anxiety or depression that are impacting your daily life, seeking help from a mental health professional is recommended. Similarly, if you're struggling with addiction or substance abuse, seeking help from a professional can be life-changing. Additionally, if you have a physical condition that requires medical attention, seeking help from a healthcare professional is essential.

One of the most effective forms of professional help for mental health issues is therapy. Therapy can help individuals develop coping mechanisms, identify and change negative thought patterns, and improve communication skills. There are many different types of therapy, including cognitive-behavioral therapy (CBT), dialectical behavior therapy (DBT), and psychodynamic therapy, among others. Each type of therapy has its own unique approach and can be helpful for different individuals and situations.

In some cases, medication may also be necessary to manage symptoms of mental illness. Medication should always be prescribed by a healthcare professional and should be taken as directed.

When seeking professional help, it's important to find the right professional for your needs. This may involve researching different professionals in your area, asking for recommendations from friends or family members, or speaking with your primary care physician. It's also important to feel comfortable with the professional you choose and to communicate openly about your needs and concerns.

Remember, seeking professional help is not a sign of weakness but rather a courageous step towards improving your well-being.

In addition to therapy and medication, there are other forms of professional help that can be beneficial for overall health and well-being. For example, seeking the help of a nutritionist or dietitian can be helpful for individuals struggling with diet-related health issues or looking to improve their overall diet. Similarly, seeking the help of a personal trainer or fitness coach can be helpful for individuals looking to improve their physical health and fitness.

Additionally, there are various types of alternative therapies that can be beneficial for individuals looking for non-traditional forms of professional help. These may include acupuncture, massage therapy, yoga, and mindfulness practices. It's important to note that while these alternative therapies may be helpful for some individuals, they should not be used as a substitute for traditional medical treatment when necessary.

Ultimately, seeking professional help is a courageous and important step towards improving one's overall health and well-being. It's important to remember that seeking help is a sign of strength and resilience, and there is no shame in reaching out for support when needed.

In addition to seeking professional help for mental health issues, it's also important to seek help for physical health problems. This may involve seeing a doctor, physical therapist, or other healthcare professionals. It's important to take your physical health seriously and seek help when needed.

It's also important to remember that seeking help is not a sign of weakness. It takes strength and courage to recognize when you need help and to take action to improve your health and well-being. Seeking help is a sign of self-care and shows that you are willing to prioritize your health and happiness.

In this chapter, you'll learn about different types of professionals who can help with mental and physical health issues, as well as tips on how to find the right professional for your needs. You'll also learn about the different types of treatments that may be available, such as therapy, medication, and lifestyle changes, and how to navigate the process of seeking professional help.

Chapter 12: Embrace Change for Personal Growth

Change is inevitable in life, and learning to embrace it can lead to personal growth and development. In this chapter, we'll explore the benefits of embracing change and provide practical tips on how to adapt to change. We'll discuss the impact of resilience, flexibility, and positive thinking on personal growth.

1. Understanding the different types of change: Change can come in various forms such as planned, unplanned, positive, negative, internal, or external. Learning how to identify and categorize the different types of change can help us better understand and embrace them.

2. Building resilience: Resilience is the ability to bounce back from difficult situations. It involves developing a positive mindset, maintaining strong social connections, and practicing self-care. Building resilience can help us navigate change more effectively and grow from it.

3. Learning from past experiences: Looking back on past experiences of change can help us understand how we have coped in the past and what we can do differently in the future. Reflecting on what we have learned and how we have grown from previous experiences of change can also help us build resilience.

4. Developing flexibility: Being open-minded and adaptable can help us adjust to new situations and experiences. Developing flexibility involves being willing to try new things, being open to different perspectives, and being able to pivot when necessary.

5. Embracing uncertainty: Change often brings uncertainty, which can be uncomfortable and anxiety-provoking. However, learning to embrace uncertainty and see it as an opportunity for growth can help us build resilience and adaptability.

6. Setting goals: Setting goals can help us focus on the positive aspects of change and give us something to work towards. It can also help us break down big changes into smaller, more manageable steps.

7. Seeking support: Change can be overwhelming, and it's essential to seek support from friends, family, or professionals when needed. Talking to others about our experiences and feelings can help us process change and develop coping strategies.

Chapter 13: Connect with Nature for Mental and Physical Health

Connecting with nature can have a significant impact on mental and physical health. In this chapter, we'll explore the benefits of spending time in nature and provide guidance on how to incorporate nature into daily life. We'll discuss the impact of outdoor activities, gardening, and eco-therapy on health and well-being.

Spending time in nature has been linked to reduced stress, improved mood, increased creativity, and better physical health. In this chapter, readers will learn about the various benefits of connecting with nature and the importance of incorporating it into their daily lives.

The chapter will cover different ways to connect with nature, such as going for a walk in the park, taking up gardening, or participating in outdoor activities like hiking or camping. The benefits of eco-therapy, which involves spending time in natural environments as a form of therapy, will also be discussed.

Additionally, the chapter will provide practical tips on how to overcome barriers to connecting with nature, such as lack of time or access to outdoor spaces. Readers will learn how to make small changes in their daily routines to incorporate more time in nature and reap the benefits for their mental and physical health.

Spending time in nature has also been linked to improved cognitive function and creativity. Studies have shown that spending time in natural environments can lead to improved attention and memory, as well as increased creativity and problem-solving skills. Additionally, exposure to natural environments has been found to reduce symptoms of attention deficit hyperactivity disorder (ADHD) in children and adults.

Moreover, connecting with nature has been shown to reduce stress and improve mood. Being in nature can lower levels of the stress hormone cortisol and increase levels of the feel-good hormone serotonin. This can lead to reduced feelings of anxiety and depression, and improved overall emotional well-being.

In this chapter, we'll explore different ways to connect with nature and reap its benefits for mental and physical health. We'll discuss the benefits of outdoor activities, such as hiking and camping, and provide guidance on how to incorporate nature into daily life, such as by creating a nature-inspired home environment or practicing mindfulness in nature.

In addition to the benefits of outdoor activities, gardening, and eco-therapy, this chapter could also delve into the concept of biophilia - the innate human connection with nature. It could explore how being in nature can reduce stress, anxiety, and depression and increase feelings of happiness and overall well-being. The chapter could also provide practical tips on how to spend more time in nature, even for those living in urban areas, such as visiting parks, taking walks in green spaces, or incorporating indoor plants into their living spaces. Additionally, the chapter could touch upon the importance of preserving natural environments and protecting biodiversity for the benefit of both humans and the planet.

Chapter 14: Practice Gratitude for Emotional Health

Practicing gratitude can have a significant impact on emotional health and well-being. In this chapter, we'll explore the benefits of gratitude and provide practical tips on how to cultivate a grateful mindset. We'll discuss the impact of gratitude journaling, expressing gratitude to others, and focusing on the present moment.

Expressing gratitude is an essential component of positive psychology that helps cultivate a sense of appreciation for what we have in our lives. In this chapter, we will explore the benefits of practicing gratitude and how it can improve emotional health.

First, we will discuss the impact of gratitude on mental health and well-being. Studies have shown that individuals who practice gratitude report higher levels of positive emotions, better sleep quality, and reduced stress levels. Practicing gratitude can also lead to increased optimism and resilience, which can help individuals cope with life's challenges.

Next, we will provide practical tips on how to cultivate a grateful mindset. These include gratitude journaling, which involves writing down things you are grateful for each day, expressing gratitude to others, and focusing on the present moment. We will also discuss the importance of being mindful of negative thoughts and focusing on positive aspects of life.

Finally, we will discuss how to incorporate gratitude into daily life. This includes setting reminders to express gratitude throughout the day, practicing gratitude in social situations, and incorporating gratitude practices into daily routines.

Overall, this chapter will provide valuable insights and techniques on how to cultivate gratitude and improve emotional health.

Gratitude can also help improve relationships with others, as expressing gratitude towards others can increase feelings of positivity and connectedness. In addition, cultivating a grateful mindset can help individuals to cope with stress and difficult situations, as it can provide perspective and a sense of appreciation for what one already has.

Furthermore, research has shown that practicing gratitude can have physical health benefits as well. For example, it has been linked to improved sleep quality, lower blood pressure, and decreased symptoms of depression.

In this chapter, we will explore specific techniques for practicing gratitude and incorporating it into daily life, as well as discuss the various benefits it can have for both emotional and physical health.

some techniques for practicing gratitude:

1. Gratitude journaling: Set aside time each day to write down three things you are grateful for. This can help shift your focus towards the positive aspects of your life.

2. Gratitude letters: Write a letter expressing gratitude to someone who has positively impacted your life. This can help strengthen your relationships and increase feelings of happiness and well-being.

3. Mindful gratitude: Practice being present in the moment and focusing on the things around you that you are grateful for. This can be as simple as taking a moment to appreciate a beautiful sunset or a kind gesture from a friend.

4. Gratitude jar: Write down things you are grateful for on small pieces of paper and put them in a jar. When you're feeling down, pull out a few pieces of paper and read them to remind yourself of the good things in your life.

5. Gratitude meditation: Set aside time to meditate and focus on feelings of gratitude. This can help increase feelings of calm and contentment.

By practicing gratitude regularly, you can improve your emotional health and overall well-being.

Chapter 15: Foster Creativity for Personal Expression

Fostering creativity can be a powerful tool for personal expression and self-discovery. In this chapter, we'll explore the benefits of creativity and provide guidance on how to nurture creative expression. We'll discuss the impact of art, music, and writing on personal growth and development.

Creativity is an essential aspect of self-expression and can have a profound impact on personal growth and development. In Chapter 15, we will delve into the benefits of creativity and provide practical tips on how to nurture your creative side.

We will begin by exploring the impact of creativity on mental health and well-being. Research has shown that engaging in creative activities can help reduce stress, anxiety, and depression. It can also improve overall cognitive function, including memory, problem-solving, and decision-making skills.

Next, we will provide guidance on how to foster creativity in everyday life. We will discuss various creative outlets, such as painting, drawing, photography, and music, and provide tips on how to incorporate them into your daily routine. We will also explore the benefits of journaling, writing, and storytelling as creative forms of self-expression.

Finally, we will discuss the importance of experimentation and taking risks in fostering creativity. We will explore the idea that creativity is not limited to traditional artistic pursuits and can be expressed in various ways, such as problem-solving, innovation, and entrepreneurship.

By the end of this chapter, readers will have a better understanding of the benefits of creativity and practical tips on how to nurture their creative side to enhance personal expression and self-discovery.

Benefit of creativity

- The benefits of creativity extend beyond personal expression and can also include stress relief, improved cognitive function, and increased self-esteem.

- Creativity can take many forms, and individuals may find that certain forms of creative expression resonate more with them than others. For example, some people may find that they enjoy visual arts such as painting or photography, while others may prefer writing or playing music.

- Nurturing creativity can involve setting aside time for creative pursuits, experimenting with different forms of expression, and seeking out sources of inspiration.

- For those who may be hesitant to express themselves creatively, it can be helpful to remember that there is no "right" or "wrong" way to create, and that the process of creating can be just as valuable as the end result.

- Finally, it's worth noting that while creative expression can be a powerful tool for personal growth, it's important not to put pressure on oneself to produce "perfect" or "successful" works of art. Instead, the focus should be on the act of creating itself and the benefits that can come from engaging in that process.

Chapter 16: Establish Financial Health for Overall Well-Being

Establishing financial health is essential for overall well-being. In this chapter, we'll explore the benefits of financial stability and provide practical tips on how to improve financial health. We'll discuss the impact of budgeting, saving, and investing on mental and physical health.

In today's fast-paced world, financial stability is critical for overall well-being. In this chapter, we will delve into the importance of financial health and explore ways to establish it.

Financial instability can lead to stress, anxiety, and other mental health issues. Hence, it is essential to manage your finances properly to avoid such problems. We will discuss the impact of budgeting and how it can help you manage your expenses effectively. We will also provide practical tips on how to create a budget and stick to it.

Saving money is another crucial aspect of financial health. We will explore the benefits of saving money and provide practical tips on how to save money effectively. We will also discuss the importance of setting financial goals and how to achieve them.

Investing is another crucial aspect of financial health. We will explore the benefits of investing and provide guidance on how to invest your money wisely. We will also discuss the impact of investing on your overall financial health and well-being.

In addition to the above, we will discuss the importance of understanding your financial situation and making informed financial decisions. We will provide guidance on how to manage debt, improve your credit score, and make the most of your money.

Overall, this chapter will provide you with the necessary tools and knowledge to establish financial health and achieve overall well-being.

We'll also provide guidance on how to manage debt and avoid financial stress. We'll discuss the importance of setting financial goals, tracking expenses, and developing a financial plan. Additionally, we'll explore the impact of financial literacy and education on long-term financial health. Overall, this chapter will provide valuable insights and strategies for achieving financial stability and promoting overall well-being

Managing debt and avoiding financial stress is crucial for achieving financial health and overall well-being. Here are some guidance and tips on how to manage debt and avoid financial stress:

1. Create a budget: Creating a budget is essential for managing debt and avoiding financial stress. Start by tracking your income and expenses, then identify areas where you can cut back on unnecessary expenses.

2. Prioritize debt payments: Prioritize paying off high-interest debts first, such as credit card debts or payday loans. Make minimum payments on other debts while focusing on paying off the highest interest debts as quickly as possible.

3. Consider debt consolidation: Debt consolidation involves combining multiple debts into one manageable monthly payment with a lower interest rate. This can make it easier to pay off debts and reduce financial stress.

4. Avoid new debt: Avoid taking on new debt while paying off existing debt. This means avoiding unnecessary purchases and using credit cards responsibly.

5. Seek help when needed: If you're struggling with debt and financial stress, seek help from a financial advisor or credit counselor. They can provide guidance on how to manage debt and create a plan to achieve financial health.

In Conclusion

Living a healthy life is a continuous journey that requires commitment and dedication. By following the essential rules outlined in this book, you can create a fulfilling and healthy life that allows you to reach your full potential. Remember, taking care of your physical, mental, and emotional health is essential for overall well-being. So, start today and take small steps towards a healthier life.

This book has explored various aspects of personal growth and well-being. We have delved into the importance of physical health, emotional well-being, intellectual growth, and financial stability. We have learned that making small changes in our daily lives can have a significant impact on our overall health and happiness.

We have seen that incorporating habits such as exercise, healthy eating, and mindfulness can improve physical health and reduce the risk of chronic diseases. We have explored the impact of positive emotions such as gratitude, kindness, and humor on emotional health and how creativity and nature can aid in self-discovery and personal expression.

We have also discussed the benefits of continuous learning, seeking professional help when needed, and embracing change for personal growth. Finally, we have explored the impact of financial stability on overall well-being and provided practical tips on how to improve financial health.

Overall, this book has provided a holistic approach to personal growth and well-being, emphasizing that our physical, emotional, intellectual, and financial health are all interconnected. By making small changes in our daily lives, we can improve our overall health and happiness, leading to a more fulfilling and rewarding life.